MR M S Lewis

The Relevance of Church Based, Compared to Non Church Based, Youth Groups in Todays Society
What's The Point in Youth Groups?

First Produced 2012

First Published 2012 in the UK by The University of Wales Newport, UK

Second Edition Published 2013 in the UK by Adventure Press Ltd

 www.theAdventurePress.com

ISBN-13: 978-1492930211

First Published On Behalf Of
The University of Wales, Newport
School of Sport, Health and Applied Social Sciences
2012

The Relevance of Church Based, Compared to Non Church Based, Youth Groups in Todays Society What's The Point in Youth Groups?

MR M S Lewis

First Produced 2012 under the title

Evaluation of the relevance of Church Based Youth Groups in todays society in Comparison to non Church Based Youth Groups

ABSTRACT

EVALUATION OF THE RELEVANCE OF CHURCH BASED YOUTH GROUPS IN TODAY'S SOCIETY IN COMPARISON TO NON CHURCH BASED YOUTH GROUPS

My research is based on two different types of youth groups; church based and non church based. I met up with Christian youth and non Christian youth groups, interviewing and meeting both young people and the leaders.

In hindsight the question I posed was too big for the sample group I studied. It was clear that both types of group have merits and focused on their young people. It was apparent that agendas set by each group were influenced by external bodies and organizations linking to funding and governance.

The main question of whether these types of youth groups are relevant has been answered and it is clear that the young people find these groups relevant and beneficial in their lives to some degree.

Table of Contents

Chapter 1

Introduction

This projects aim was to evaluate the relevance of Christian youth groups in today's society in comparison to non Christian youth groups.

This research represents the culmination of a two and a half month research project into the relevance of youth work in both Church and non Church based groups. It is well documented that youth work evolved through the churches and faith based movements. Until the early 20th century youth work was predominantly a form of letting young working men whom had left their homes to work in the cities and needed somewhere to socialize meet up with other young people.

One of the first youth organizations setup in the UK was the YMCA in 1844, followed closely by the Boys Brigade. The women's version of these seemed less relevant at the time and as such it wasn't until 1878 when Maude Stanley developed the Girls Club Union to address the imbalance and assist young girls.

Lily Montagu setup in 1896 the children's Synagogue Services in London which has now evolved into the organization know as UK Youth.

In 1907 Robert Baden Powell famously setup the Scouting movement and followed this in 1910 with the Girl Guides.

All these organizations were based on Christian morals and the aim of these groups was to provide both emotional and spiritual support alongside the physical needs of young men.

In 1960 after some concerns amongst the general public on teenage delinquency a report was prepared for Government that was to change youth work forever. The Albermarle Report was released which outlined a statutory youth sector for the UK. This introduced paid youth workers and youth centers across the country which were not fundamentally based on christian morals. (Smith, 1988)

And there we have the fundamental reason for this research. Both styles of youth work continued from this point with the Christian based organizations drifting further from the statutory based youth work.

"To cap my personal "philosophy of youthwork," I start with the culture of youth. Youth are their own entity with their own culture that adults must recognize and validate. Youth work is not only an opportunity for adults to better understand their "being," but includes active involvement in validating young people and their culture. You are not doing youth work unless you are learning something from the young people. Unfortunately, so many adults do not understand that young people are their own culture and discriminate against them accordingly." (Whittaker, 2000)

By looking at changes in the philosophies underpinning youth work, it is clear that life has changed dramatically from when I was a young person to the life a lot of young people have today.

The philosophy of youth work post the world war period was appropriate in an age of rapid and fairly predictable transitions but does not address the more complex and protracted extended transitions of contemporary youth and also ignores other changes such as the lowering of the average age of puberty and the impact of the media. In other words, the main models of youth work were developed at a time when the client group was much more clearly defined. (Krieger, 1996)

One measure of relevance relates to the extent to which youth work remains attractive and meets the needs of the different age groups of young people as they face complex decisions and challenging economic circumstances.

It will be crucial to this research that my own beliefs and that the 'faith' aspect does not be a main focus on this research, but that the church based and non church based youth work be the dividing line to see the relevance to the young people. It would be fair to assume that young people going to a church based youth group would have links to a faith, albeit on the other hand young people attending non church based groups will not be excluded from saying they have a faith or not.

So what if anything, can a Church based Youth Work approach offer young people who have no faith or are from different religious traditions? Is there anything that can be drawn from the Christian intellectual and spiritual heritage to benefit young people who are not interested in Church based belief and cultures?

This study will focus on evidence and research to be carried out within two locations in Rhondda Cynon Taff and create a conclusion to my question about the relevance of Christian youth groups in today's society in comparison to non Christian youth groups.

I want to see if either is better than the other and whether peoples perspective is that one is more relevant than the other. I want to see if either has a better morale standing and better morale basis for doing what they do and exactly what benefit Church based may or may not have over non church based youth work.

Drawing on information from the young people and youth group leaders, I will examine the effectiveness of church based and non church based youth groups in developing citizenship skills among the young people through discussion. I will also assess the level of association between the objectives of providers and those of the users in order to assess the view of Hendry and colleagues (1992) that there is often a mismatch between the aims and objectives of youth work providers and those who use their facilities.

Chapter 2

Literature Review

Historically youth work has taken many forms starting from Sunday Schools associated with churches and chapels in the last few years of the eighteenth century, and, in particular, the activities of pioneers such as Robert Raikes and Hannah More as an important forerunner of the work. Young Men's Christian Association (YMCA), set up in 1844, was the first dedicated youth organization. In the late eighteen century the establishment of the scouts association gave young people means to live in the wilderness and learn practical skills in a fun and challenging environment. Later in the century the making of clubs and centers became a major way of working with young people, here the work of the Reverend Arthur Sweatman is of special note. He had been involved in setting up and running a youth's institute and had looked at the activities of a number of similar initiatives. In a paper read to the Social Science Association in Edinburgh in October 1863 he made one of the first cases for specific provision for youth (via clubs and institutes)

"Their peculiar wants are evening recreation, companionship, an entertaining but healthy literature, useful instruction, and a strong guiding influence to lead them onward and upward socially and morally; their dangers are, the long evenings consequent upon early closing, the unrestraint they are allowed at home, the temptations of the streets and of their time of life, and a little money at the bottom of their pockets." (Sweatman 1879)

Modern day youth work approaches have moved away from Christian based youth work unlike in the early 18th and 19th centuries as the church played a great part in creating a faith based approach in working with the youth. This some times had an evangelical undertone and some times was there to provide help or recreational activities for the young people so they may stay off the streets and out of trouble.

Today's youth work approaches are still vaguely based on what Reverend Arthur Sweatman said in his paper to the Social Science Association in Edinburgh in October 1879. But most of what is seen as youth work practice can be identified from what has been happening in differing degrees in the central discourses of the practice since the early 1900s (Doyle and Smith, 1999).

So youth work involves the following key principals

- Focus on young people (Jeffs and Smith 1998)
- Emphasizing voluntary participation and relationship the voluntary principle, as Tony Jeffs (2001) has commented, this has distinguished youth work from most other services provided for this age group. Young people have, traditionally, been able to freely enter into relationships with workers and to end those relationships when they want. This has fundamental implications for the way in which youth workers operate and the opportunities open to them. It can encourage youth workers to think and work in rather more dialogical ways
- Committing to association- joining together in companionship or to undertake some task, and the educative power of playing one's part in a group or association (Doyle and Smith 1999)
- Being friendly and informal, and acting with integrity as Josephine Macalister Brew (1957) put it, 'young people want to know where they are and they need the friendship of those who have confidence and faith'. It follows from this that the settings workers help to build should be convivial, the relationships they form honest and characterized by 'give and take'; and the programs they are involved in, flexible. 'A youth leader must try not to be too concerned about results', Brew wrote, 'and at all costs not to be over-anxious').
- Being concerned with the education and, more broadly, the welfare of young people.

All of these five elements make up the back bone of twentieth century youth work and it dose not matter if the youth work is Christian, Jewish, Hindu, secular or Church based based work as all are providing a generic service for all young people.

According to Pope John Paul II (1995) the young people are a sign of hope for the church, country and humanity , which is the desire of every priest, pastor or any religious leader. Not only does the young person need to be a sign of hope and light, they also need to be a sign of life in the church. Being a young people is a time in one's life wherein there is a lot of energy. A church which has a lot of involvement for the young people, is a church that is full of life.

In one of Pope Benedict XVI messages in the Vatican, he mentioned a metaphor of a plant that grows firm on a foundation of strong roots. He asked young people in his message for World Youth Day 2011 to strengthen their faith to counter the influence of secular society. The presence of young people, he wrote, "renews, rejuvenates and gives new energy to the Church." The Church, he wrote, is depending on the young people of the world. "She needs your lively faith, your creative charity and the energy of your hope." "Your presence renews, rejuvenates and gives new energy to the Church. (Catholic News Agency 2011)

But there seem to be a growing number of young people that are uninterested towards the church. There has been a growing interest of the young people toward surfing the internet. According to researchers with the National Study of Youth and Religion, the vast majority of teens, ages 13 to 17, have access to the Internet and spend on average nearly 7 hours a week surfing the web. This means that the average teen is probably spending more time on the Internet each week than participating in religious activities and this can cause concerns on the young persons well being. (National Study of Youth and Religion sited in Smith et al, 2011).

This seems to be a conservative study of the average time a young person spends surfing the web every week. Some studies indicate that it even reaches up to almost 12 hours a week. According to George Colony the CEO of Forrester Research, in a talk to Forbes magazine in 2010, the amount of time young people spend on the Internet has increased 121% since 2005 over the last five years and the internet use is 12 hours per week for18-30 year olds.

In that same message given by the pope mentioned earlier, he also added that in a contemporary culture that has the tendency to exclude God and consider faith only relevant to the private sphere, he encouraged young people to strengthen their faith, exclaiming, "You are the future of society and of the Church!" (Catholic News Agency, 2011)

The question of how to attract and sustain the young people into the church is one major concern during this troubled age for church based youth groups. In a time where technological advancement is at its peak; Ipod, MTV, internet, facebook, computer games and many others, the church is in a tight battle for the attention of young people.

The involvement of the young people in the church maybe an avenue for their transformation in becoming responsible and godly citizens. Pope Benedict XVI said, "... wherever individuals and nations accept God's presence, worship him in truth and listen to his voice, then the civilization of love is being built, a civilization in which the dignity of all is respected, and communion increases, with all its benefits." (Catholic News Agency ,2011)

This is the reason why surveys will be conducted to find out the young people's view and experience of the church so that the church may evaluate its present activities and gain an insight in making certain adjustments to enhance its approach, activities and programs for the young people.

The purpose of present activities and programs of the church for young people are conducted to encourage them to involve themselves in the church, but there is also a need to look on the reason why young people involves or does not involve themselves in the church. The question of what their personal reasons and motivations on their involvement still remains unclear and should be classified. This study hopes that it will be helpful in uncovering some of the reasons for young people's involvement or non-involvement in the church.

Furrow and Wagener (2000), suggested that religious adolescents report consistently higher numbers of developmental assets associated with increased restraint and decreased risk behavior. Furrow and Wagener join a long list of scholars who have found an association between religious perception and religious participation and reduced engagement in risk behaviors ranging from drug and alcohol abuse (Gorsuch, 1995; Kharari and Harmon, 1984; McBrideet al., 1996) to juvenile delinquency (Benda, 1995; Cochran, 1989; Stark et al.,1982). (2004). Smith and Faris (2002) found that regular religious service attendance, high subjective importance of faith and years spent in religious youth groups are clearly associated with high self-esteem and positive self-attitudes.

Church based youth work theoretically is a faith sensitive approach which is based on good social and personal values taken from the intellectual and spiritual heritage of faith and human Knowledge. It recognizes and accepts all spiritual dimensions and needs of people's lives with a non-judgemental and open minded attitude. It specializes in promoting support and development of Church based youth.

In practice and delivery Church based youth work should promote the same elements as generic youth work

- Developing informal education opportunities
- Delivering targeted support for specific young people
- Planning and providing positive activities for young people (places to go and things to do)
- Supporting young people participation in decision making
- Providing Information, Advice and Guidance
- Detached and street based youth work
- Promotes integration and social cohesion
- Empowerment of young people

From this it can be clearly deduced a Church based youth approach can be beneficial for all individuals regardless of having faith or not. The basic needs of all humans are the same, Physical, safety, affection; esteem and self actualization (Maslow 1947) these needs are not faith, creed or no faith specific but are for all of Humanity.

Church based youth works intellectual and spiritual heritage

Church based youth organizations traditionally gave utmost importance to the training of children and youth in the education of the individual. Historically Church based scholars have done much good work in the area of child development, child psychology and youth Education.

Amongst the many Church based scholars who have written on the education of children, are Ibn Sina, Ibn Khaldun and Al-Ghazali, Tim Neufeld, Mark Senter and Andy Hawthorne.

Historically church based youth groups wanted to start educating their children, and change their sinful nature (Senter, 2010). Sunday schools started hundreds of years ago, before child labor laws. Children were working during the week, and on Sundays they were not doing anything productive and people were worried. The pastors at local churches generally treated young people no differently than they did adults. Many parents did not want their children to attend the Sunday school for fear of persecution.

During the early 19th century, adults wanted to establish Bible lessons to keep young people out of trouble, and this evolved into young people having their own church service separate from adults. Church ministers began to treat the young people as young adults, but not equal to adults (Senter 2010). One current trend in some churches is having the young people in the same group as adults for part of the time, and then separate for the other part of the lesson. Youth leaders today are very active in youth ministry and the young people are still allowed to behave like young people, rather than as adults.

Whether in a separate Church based youth group, or following a newer model of attending church with adults, many young people are not continuing this lifestyle for the long-term. Hundreds of years ago Church based youth groups may have been developed to teach kids how to read the Bible, and to keep them out of trouble, today church based youth groups have an underlying mission to develop disciples for Christ. The Christian young people of today are to understand the Bible, have a relationship with Christ, and to evangelize. (Hawthorne, 1999)

Many church based youth groups are succeeding while the young people are in high school, and after they graduate they are falling off track (Bryant, 2008). According to Bryant, the attendance of young people starts to fall after each birthday. There are more 13 & 14yr olds then 15 & 16yr olds, and 18+ yr olds are the least likely to attend. Overall, after they reach aged 18 it just dwindles.

If we look back at the Bible, the traditions and life of Jesus, we find a clear blueprint for later scholars to develop and create theories and practices which became milestones for modern day usages in education, child rearing, parental or guardian skills and human psychological, spiritual and physical growth.

The main methods shown and used in the education of young people can be put into four groups as follows:

1. Addressing the emotions and needs of the young people
2. Avoiding embarrassing young people
3. Being tolerant and gentle towards young people
4. Attracting their attention by asking questions

All of the above can be mistaken for social work or youth work practices in attracting and working with young people. The scholars would say of young people, they are the bearers of the religion so they should be given more attention and encouragement (Hawthorne 1999).

In 1993 in Prospects: the quarterly review of comparative education (Paris, UNESCO: International Bureau of Education), the Educational and child development methods of Ibn Khaldune the great Church based sociologist and Ibn Sina (Avicenna) the writer of the worldly renowned book on medicine "the canon" were published, in which Ibn Sina looks at the four stages of human intellectual growth from being in the mothers womb all the way to adulthood. According to Beilin (1994) this is similar to Jean Piagets theory of cognitive development

- The infant stage: (from birth until the second year) Avicenna's concern with the child begins from birth. 'When he is born, the child's umbilical cord must be cut at once, above four fingers' length, and tied with clean, fine wool twisted lightly, so as not to cause pain; if we wish to swaddle him, then the midwife must first massage his limbs gently; she must inspect his body where this is necessary, moving every limb into the best position; all of this by gentle touching with the tips of her fingers which should become a regular habit, and she should often wipe his eyes with silk or something similar'.
- The stage of childhood: this lasts from the third to the fifth year, at the time when 'the child's body strengthens, his tongue is free, and he is ready for instruction, and his hearing is attentive'
- The first stage of teaching this begins at the age of 6 and ends approximately at 14 years of age. It is on reaching this age that the child must begin receiving education of a more serious kind, gradually moving away from games and sport, and beginning organized study. 'Until [children] complete their fourteenth year, they must gradually decrease their sporting activities
- The specialized education stage (age 14 onwards) This comes after the child has completed general primary teaching, and his aptitudes have become apparent either to continue in the field of education or to learn a craft and earn a living. In the light of these aptitudes, the young person defines for himself the type of study or the type of vocational work that appeals to him during the higher or specialized stage. (Prospect: 1993)

So basically we see that at birth we are entirely devoid of knowledge; we are still no more than 'raw material'. We then gradually gain 'form' 'thanks to the knowledge we acquire through our organs'. Essentially ignorant, we fulfil ourselves as human beings only through knowledge. This is distinguished through three types of knowledge corresponding known as many 'degrees of thought'.

There is practical knowledge, the product of 'the discerning intelligence', which allows us to act in the world in a controlled fashion; then 'a knowledge of what we must or must not do and of what is good or evil', which we acquire through our 'empirical intelligence' and which guides us in our relations with our fellows; and, lastly, theoretical knowledge of everything that exists in the world, which we conquer by our 'speculative intelligence'. Only this last type of knowledge, the subject of the sciences, gives us the possibility of reaching perfection of soul. (Prospect 1993)

In reading the works of these Church based scholars, it was clear that over a thousand years of study is still in use in nurseries, schools, educational institutes and youth centers around the world even though they might not know it.

Young people spend a great deal of time thinking about, talking about, and being in romantic relationships (Furman, 2002), yet adults typically dismiss adolescent dating relationships as superficial. Young people do not agree: half of all teens report having been in a dating relationship and nearly one-third of all teens said they have been in a serious relationship (Teenage Research Unlimited, 2006).

Although most adolescent relationships last for only a few weeks or months, these early relationships play a pivotal role in the lives of adolescents and are important to developing the capacity for long-term, committed relationships in adulthood. The quality of adolescent romantic relationships can have long lasting effects on self-esteem and shape personal values regarding romance, intimate relationships, and sexuality (Barber & Eccles, 2003)

Romantic relationships become increasingly significant in the lives of young people as they move from early to late adolescence. Although dating has not yet begun, in early adolescence (ages 10-14) most young people are very preoccupied with romantic issues. Young people at this age spend significant amounts of time in mixed-gender groups that intensify their romantic interest and may eventually lead to romantic relationships (Connolly, Craig, Goldberg, & Pepler, 2004). Romantic relationships are central to social life during middle to late adolescence (ages 15-19). Three-fourths of teens age 16-18 report having had a relationship, dated, or "hooked up" with someone and half of these young people have had a serious boyfriend or girlfriend (Teenage Research Unlimited, 2006). Many young people in middle to late adolescence report spending more time with their romantic partner than with friends and family (Furman & Schaffer, 2003).

Chapter 3

Methodology

This study covers only two areas of Rhondda Cynon Taff and specifically a church based youth group and a non church based youth group in both Porth and Pontypridd. The research was meant to be primarily focused on young people aged thirteen to eighteen. In each neighborhood the project examined young peoples and service providers' experiences of youth work within both Church based and non church based situations.

These youth groups agreed to participate in the study on the basis that they be kept anonymous from the actual text of the research. These particular groups were chosen because youth involvement has always been a problem in these areas for several years. The result of this study would greatly benefit the youth leaders that they will consider the reasons and motivation for church based and non church based involvement of the youth when formulating youth activities in their areas. Therefore the research will be limited by the locales and the number of willing participants.

One thing I have to emphasis at the start which I didn't consider in my planning documentation but has come to light and relevance almost as soon as I started meeting people and talking to them is that the areas I have chosen are considered impoverished and are recognized by Europe as an Objective one area which means that some of these young people I am working with to complete this research are vulnerable young people. That has become an underlying tone to my research and sadly it would seem that some people wear it like a label.

In this study I adopted an empirical approach using both the qualitative and quantitative approaches used to evaluate the relevance of Church based and non church youth work were based in two areas in which young people are potentially attending youth groups and the areas are classed as category one regions and that classes the young people as in areas of poverty and potential vulnerability. In each area I visited a Church based and non church youth program and interviewed the youth leader. I also carried out questionnaires on 8 young people in each group and then interviewed 2 young people in each group.

I wanted to know what the local residents of each area thought of the youth groups and there relevance so rather than wildly guess I met up with a local councillor in each area and questioned them on what there constituents felt about the local youth provision and its relevance. I tried to interview the Assembly Minister for lifelong learning but as of publishing my findings have been unsuccessful at gaining an interview with him.

I also wanted to get a professional opinion on the relevance of these provisions and so interviewed the local Police Community Support Officer (PCSO) in both Pontypridd and Porth to find out if they felt there was a difference in effectiveness and relevance of the various provisions in their areas.

Finally I spoke to and interviewed professional experts in the field of child protection and asked them their opinions on whether Church based and non church youth work is relevant and whether one or the other makes a difference.

I will use the qualitative method to gauge responses to generic questions about what the young people do within their youth groups and about the provision of the youth groups in interviews and face to face discussions.

By using a quantitative approach I will use factual and numerical data and compare from both types of youth group to each other. (Bell 2005). As part of this approach I am looking specifically at the questionnaires the young people completed and I compared them to each locale and each group within the locale. I will began by looking at overall patterns of involvement in any kind of youth group, uniformed organization or interest groups and then focus on differential patterns of participation between groups and at over-lapping membership. Finally, I will look at involvement with detached and outreach youth workers, comparing the information provided against the others. This will allow the young people and their youth workers to reflect on behaviors, attitudes and experiences in a semi structured process.

I asked a number of young people in each of the groups I was looking at to complete my questionnaires. It turned out that I was able to get 8 from each group to participate. Following the questionnaires I requested to interview five of the young people in each group however I was only able to get two young people from each group to go ahead with the interviews. I ended up with 15 and 16 year olds in the interviews as I struggled to get more from the groups.

By using a Qualitative method I utilized semi structured interviews I held group discussions with the two young people, each lasted up to 30 minutes and I encouraged open discussion. Non deliberately all the young people attending these discussions ended up being male so that made it easier for the young people as we were the same sex. These discussion groups complement the other data sources I have by adding a qualitative dimension and by providing the young people with the opportunity to explain and explore needs which could potentially be met through their youth group leaders. (Bell, 2005)

The final part of the research gathering was done by having the individual interviews with the young people. These interviews offered an opportunity for me to consider more subtle issues relevant to the young people who have personal experience of a range of youth activities including detached and outreach programs. To be fair these were not easy to arrange as some of the young people had trust issues, however once I was past this barrier these interviews were done with myself and the young person in a friendly environment over a coffee so that it was non intimidating and was relaxed. I had with me a colleague who observed the interview but was not intrusive into the interview. This was great as it gave me the freedom to dig a little and get more information out of the interviewee. (Berg, 2001).

A total of 8 young people were interviewed for this research.

As part of the same research I also interviewed the main leader of each group, the local PCSO and the local councillors. These people were then sent a self completion form which contained questions concerning the number of young people who attended the group, the frequency and duration of the provision, the age range, sex, and charges levied. I then tried to interview them face to face which failed due to timings and commitments which got in the way of face to face meetings. Therefor Interviews were based on the use of a schedule which sought in-depth information on a whole range of areas including; the background and training of providers; knowledge of the neighborhood and young people's situations; policy, aims and objectives; funding and resourcing, levels of involvement of young people; recording, evaluation and outcomes; and the impact of local government reorganization. Interviews were either conducted over the telephone, each lasting between 15 and 25.

I had to be careful as these interviews had potential to be biased so I had to keep in check my personal opinions and ensure that I remained neutral in my thinking and opinions. (Bell, 2005)

As part of my evidence collecting I used primary evidence such as questionnaires, interviews, group discussions and also some secondary evidence such as previous studies, third hand information by interviewing councilors and asking PCSOs for their communities thoughts and opinions.

I had to be aware of ethical considerations as part of my research as it would be unethical to conduct any of my interviewing or questionnaires without informed consent. (Haynes et al, 2003)

I believe that these methods and sources enabled me to comment on the extent to which existing Church based and non church youth work provision is being utilized by young people and whether it is relevant.

Chapter 4

Report of Findings:
Discussions & Analysis

To find out what relevance either youth group has on young people I felt I needed to interview and speak to both church based and non church based youth group leaders in four separate meetings. I had questions that were generic to all groups and then the discussions evolved from those questions and I recorded the discussions. I asked for what they thought were the top five things that influenced young people in their leisure time that the youth groups had to compete with but also that affected young peoples attitudes and behavior. I then asked them to provide how they felt the youth groups they were running was relevant to these young people and what specific relevance their youth group had to their young people.

Following my research several topics came to the forefront which have become the focus of my research.

They are;
1. Influence of External Activities.
2. Physical or Non Physical Work & Activities
3. Domestic Problems
4. Sexual Relations
5. Additional Youth Organizations Influence
6. Behaviors and Links to Crime

Below is my summations of those meetings.

Influence of External Activities.

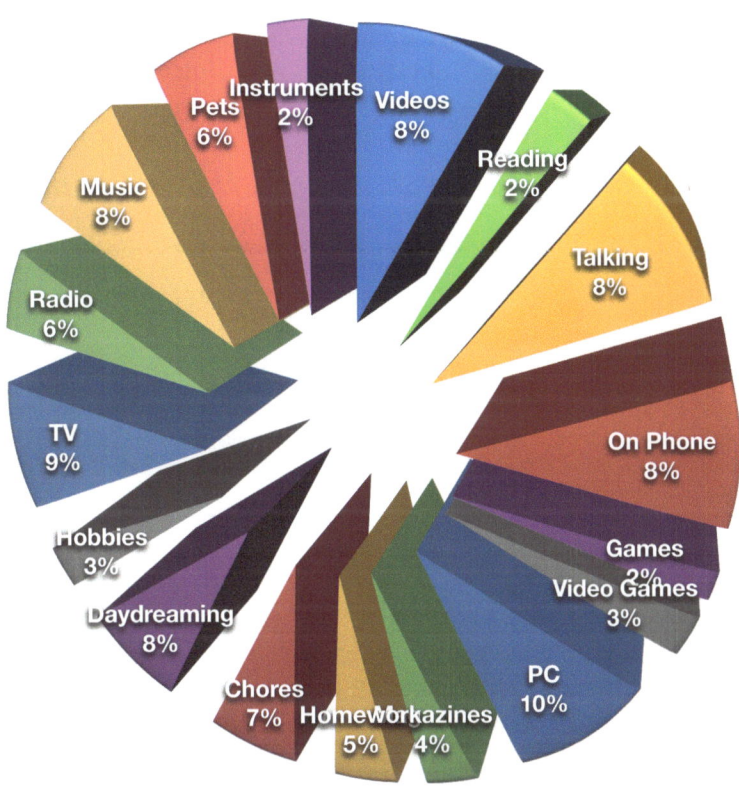

Fig 1: Young Peoples percentage of time spent on varying activities whilst at home.

After I had spoken to and interviewed the youth group leaders I then evaluated and compared the results from the young people themselves. I wanted to speak to the youth leaders to see their perspective on the young peoples time prior to reviewing my questionnaires as I didn't wish to be biased in my views or approach when I spoke to the leaders.

The questionnaires that I carried out with the young people provided the opportunity to ask a number of general questions related to young people's use of leisure time, and as seen above in Fig 1, both within and out of their homes, including modern technology, the main activities on which young people spent a lot of their free time were talking with friends, on their phones, listening to music, watching television and videos and a large percentage of their time was taken up by daydreaming.

31

The church based and the non church based youth group leaders felt that modern technology has led to the invention of personal computers, the satellite, Digital television, the internet, mobile phone (GSM) etc. The church based and the non church based youth group leaders felt that these devices have in no small measure made the world a global village. However, the challenges facing our young people is how to use them without abusing them. There was an argument between church based and non church based youth groups that these devices rather than being used for the advancement of knowledge which is capable of making the world a better place have become powerful tools for the perversion of morals. For example, both church based and non church based youth groups agree that the computer has both simplified and sped up the operation in many fields of human endeavor – data storage, medicine, architecture, music and the broadcasting industry.

Both the church based and the non church based youth group leaders agree that interactive computer software for learning of virtually any subject is excellent, that the mobile telephone has made communication easy. That satellite technology also has greatly eased the burden of real – time global communication. That the internet is a great source of information, eBooks; encyclopedias on any subject, thesis, revise, online news, libraries are now available on the internet. Various school activities which were manually carried out in the past, such as payment of school fees, access to course outlines, moodles, results etc are now done online. Sources of information and different educational operations are now available on the internet.

However both the church based and the non church based youth group leaders agree that this should be controlled and limited and that the young people should not lose sight of the bad influences that can be associated with these devices (internet, GSM and computer).

The church based youth organizations believe that many (including children, young people and even older people) are introduced to a world of deceit, indecency, immorality crime, sexual perversions, violence and many other vices through the use of these inventions of modern technology. One youth worker - Church Youth Group Leader Adult Interviewee A, also believed that "young people spend long hours watching digital videos (DVD) or playing violent, even bloody and demonic computer games".

He went on to say that in his opinion "Some young people spend hours or the whole night browsing forbidden sites on the internet thereby getting exposed to inappropriate materials, such as pornography and erotica, there is a fear that young people may get initiated into Satanism, Spiritism and other esoteric region."
He believes that the relevance of the church based youth groups is to save these young people from getting more involved in these activities and that a young person involved in his church based youth group would be guided and taught about the harm some of these modern technologies can cause. He felt that TV and internet have begun to take over the place of the bible and prayers in a good number of homes.

The church based and the non church based youth group leaders both agreed that young people treasure their wide exploration of the internet in place of reading their books and other intellectual activities. Again both the church based and the non church based youth group leaders agree that young people can be addictive in nature and, in their opinions, spend unhealthy amounts of time on their own engrossed in electronic media and activity.

The church based and the non church based youth group leaders both felt that this is potentially leading to a dramatic decline in the academic performance of the young people and a high rate of unproductively of the youth in all spheres of life.

The church based and the non church based youth group leaders both believe that parents should have more influence in addressing these challenges. One of the interviewees, Non Church Youth Group Leader Adult Interviewee B, said that "Parents should set up corrective measures to arrest this trend of self - destruction of the youth through ."

The church based and the non church based youth group leaders concluded that many young people spend long hours watching the television denying themselves of meaningful activities that will promote heathy living and advancement in life.

The church based groups believe that there is a danger within the film industry today as it presents a distorted culture which negates godly virtues. Church Youth Group Leader Adult Interviewee A said that "pre-marital sex is against God, but the film industry today presents it as the norm and what must follow or be part of a relationship" He went onto say that in his opinion "the film industry is promoting promiscuity and without restraint our young people are imbedding it as the norm."

The church based groups felt that a lot of movies are dominated with violence. In their opinion this negates Gods peaceful co-existence among men. The church based groups believe that film ratings have no effect and that businesses are happy for underage young people to see films they are too young to see as it brings in money.

Both groups agree that films can be a great experience for young people as long as they are moderated and that moderation is controlled effectively.

The Church based youth groups felt passionately that the "only way to stop this downward spiral of young people into the pit of modern technology" (Church Youth Group Leader Adult Interviewee A) was to make church more relevant to young people so that it met their spiritual, emotional and physical needs such as Robert Raikes did with the YMCA. The church based youth groups also believe that the relevance of their groups to their young people was to replace the need of external influences such as Modern technology so that young people wouldn't get distracted by "things of the world" (Church Youth Group Leader Adult Interviewee A)

On the other hand the non church based youth group leaders felt that modern technology is an integral part of modern young peoples lives and as such they needed to embrace the technology and show young people how to use it and benefit from it and at the same time make it relevant to the young persons lives. They saw their role in helping young people develop within the modern technological world rather than try and stifle young peoples interests in it. According to Non Church Youth Group Leader Adult Interviewee B, "they had a duty to nurture young peoples use of modern technology in a responsible and empowering way".

Following my questionnaires with the young people and the conversations with the youth group leaders I can see that although the youth group leaders thought the young people were up to certain things in their leisure time, they don't actually fully know their young people. It would seem that a bit of Stereotyping has developed and that the young people are not as caught up into the modern technology world that the leaders think they are into.

Physical or Non Physical Work & Activities

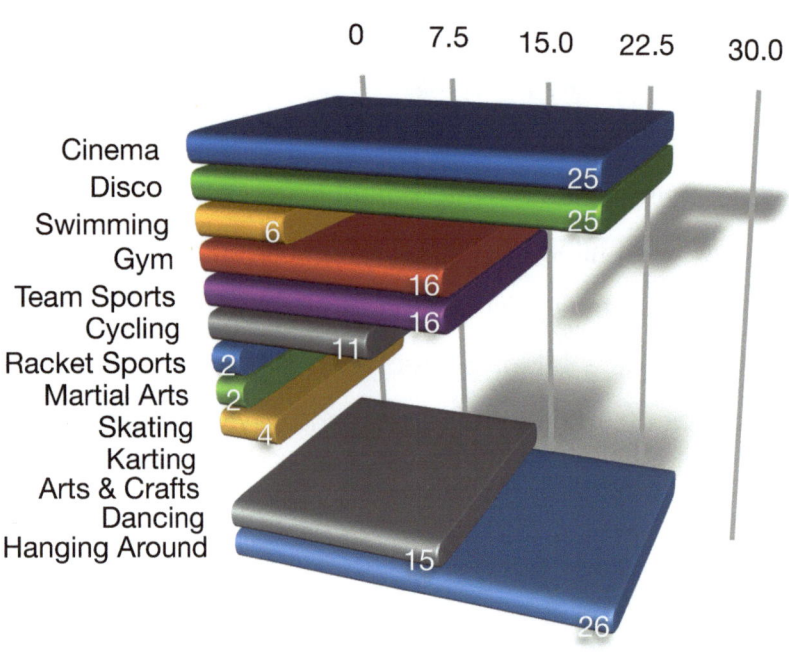

Fig 2: Young Peoples activities - physical or non-physical

Hard work is a difficult one to measure with young people. Therefore I decided to see what the young people liked doing. Whether it was based on lounging around or being participatory. My understanding of this would show me a pattern of whether the young people liked to get involved and be active or whether they liked to sit back and have an easier time.

When I examined the young peoples views on this it was interesting to see that what the information shows in Fig 2, is that the majority of them are involved in activities out of the home such as 25% of the time at the cinema, however it also shows that 25% of the time they are at discos (clubbing etc) and the biggest percentage of their time they are just hanging around with friends.

The hanging around with friends is an interesting one as it shows that potentially they have nothing better to do. So I wanted to know if they were hanging about where they were hanging about. See Fig 3 below.

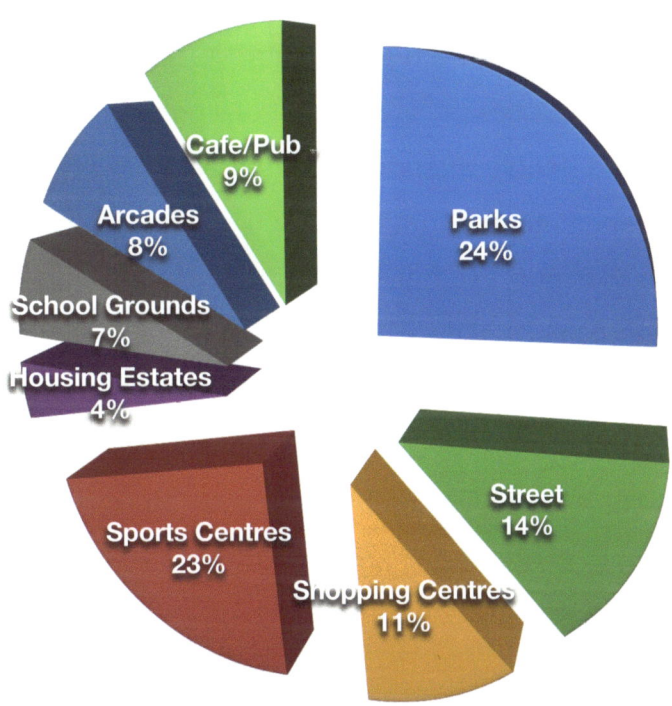

Fig 3: Percentage of time spent in varying locations whilst hanging around

It seems that the most popular place for young people to hang out with friends is in Parks or Sports centers. Upon asking them what they do in these parks the answer is sit and chill.

Within this section I have highlighted the ways in which young people use their leisure time and have drawn attention to the ways in which the transition from organized to casual leisure activities can increase vulnerability. The preference for physical social activities among young people in their mid-teens, combined with a lack of 'safe' places to pursue these activities, can lead to conflicts with the police. Fulfilling use of leisure time has positive psycho-social benefits and therefore policies which help promote active leisure life styles may ultimately reduce vulnerability and boredom. For youth work to be fully effective with young people, it is important that activities are attractive to those within the 'casual' leisure phase.

The church based and the non church based youth group leaders both felt that many of their young people want to go the easy way in life. The church based and the non church based youth group leaders both felt that young people today in their areas didn't fully grasp the concept of working hard to get what you want out of life. Both groups felt that young people wish for success in life without paying the price of diligence. It was felt that the majority of young people attending the groups have accepted the fact that they are in a social dependent state and that they will never get out of it. Both parties felt this complacency with life was a huge hurdle for young people to get over, especially in second and third generation social dependent families.

Both the church based and the non church based youth group leaders felt they had a duty to the young people to instill values and self belief, mixed with self esteem that will enable their young people to dream big and start on a journey of success enabling them to become what they want to become.

Non Church Youth Group Leader Adult Interviewee B and Church Youth Group Leader Adult Interviewee B both said that "as youth group leaders we have to show the young people that hard work pays off." Non Church Youth Group Leader Adult Interviewee B went on to say that "as a youth group we have to show young people that we are relevant, that even after a hard days work we will make the effort to turn up at the youth centre and work hard to give the young people a good time"

Church Youth Group Leader Adult Interviewee B added that "our faith gives us the strength and desire to want to be the best we can be. We use a phrase that 'excellence honors God' and we want our young people to think about that when they are doing something. Hard work is hard because we feel it and it costs us, but it makes us stronger and helps us to achieve and benefit in life giving us a better standard of living and better self esteem".

Its as Pope Benedict XVI hard work increases dignity, self esteem and a better community spirit. Both groups in the own ways reflect this and both groups believe that young people will benefit from hard work.

Its along the lines of what Maslow says, that young people can start to change their lives they will be generating their own physical, safety esteem and self actualization. The youth groups believe that they can do this by working hard to make a living for themselves.

Domestic Problems

As part of this I wanted to see the sort of family life the young people have and if that makes a difference as to what type of youth group the young people will attend. In Wales the Welsh Government produces stats that say the average unemployment in Rhondda Cynon Taff is 8.9% (www.statswales.wales.gov.uk) according to my research (chart below Fig 6) out of a possible 58 parents 44% of them are unemployed.

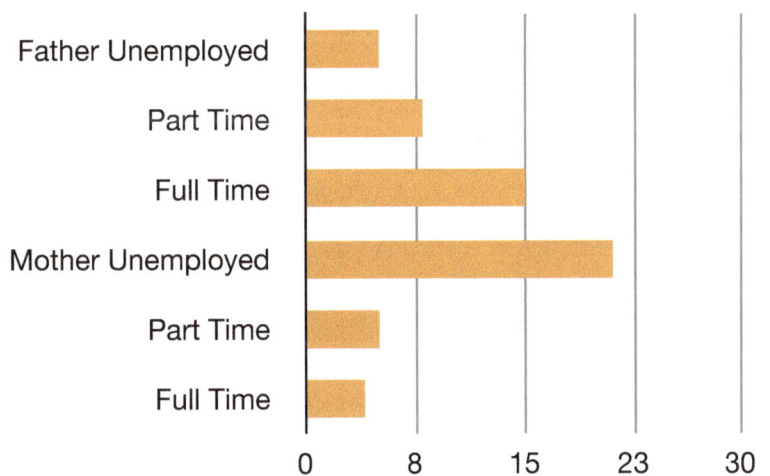

Fig 4: Unemployment/Employment Rate in Families

Low rates of economic activity among respondents' parents provides further justification for the areas selected. In all 67% of the young people I questioned lived in households without a full-time wage earner whereas the 1991 Census puts the rate of economic inactivity for Welsh households at 14%.

The majority of young people I questioned (71%) lived with two natural parents, while a further 8 per cent lived in a re-constituted, two parent family. Twenty one percent lived in a single parent family. In comparison to national figures, there is a slight over-representation of young people living in single parent families: a national survey of 10,000 young Welsh people showed that 14 per cent of young people lived with a single parent (Anderson Et al, 2009).

Of the 32 young people I questioned all are involved in a youth group (hence I was able to meet them). However all of them mention the fact that their is nowhere in their locality that actually meets their needs and is available when they need it.

Both the church based and the non church based youth group leaders agreed that many young people are confronted with domestic problems ranging from hostility from parents, strife between their fathers and mothers, parents inability to provide the basic necessities of life.

Both the church based and the non church based youth group leaders felt that young people from such homes are known to run away from home, get involved in all forms of crimes and illegal drug taking. Both groups of leaders felt that the young people often got more care and support from attending their youth groups than at home.

Church Youth Group Leader Adult Interviewee A said that "the church based groups felt that they were relevant to young people as they were able to offer more support through offering young people prayer and the opportunity to get strength from adopting a faith in Jesus."

Non Church Youth Group Leader Adult Interviewee B said that "non church based groups felt that using Jesus as a father figure was not a good option as often young peoplc felt scared or abused or neglected by their fathers. That the church based groups offered Jesus as a father figure and this could scare young people away as they couldn't relate to a 'nice' father figure." He went on to say that "Church youth groups need to get a grip on reality. Young people today cannot relate fully to a stable family background as the majority of our young people we meet and deal with are from single parent families. The support these Young People need comes in part through us and from us being there to support them and provide the guidance they need. Church groups are just not relevant when they stick a father figure into a young persons face who has no father in their lives"

This hasn't changed since Sweatman wrote about it in the 1800's - if anything with the passage of time these issues have been compounded. Domestic problems have always been an issue and always will be. Andy Hawthorne (1999) talks about how domestic issues affect young people growing up and we see here that both church and non church youth groups have a part to play in the young peoples lives as long as there is relevance and the input is morally right then linked to church or not should help the young people through Domestic issues.

Sexual Relations

The church based and the non church based youth group leaders felt that their young people do not see sexual immorality/fornication as wrong. They see it as a way of expressing their love to a person of the opposite sex. Both groups felt that the perspective of the young people is that in popular culture pre-marital sex is generally accepted. The church based youth group leaders all felt that pre martial sex has many adverse effects surrounding it.

Non Church Youth Group Leader Adult Interviewee B and Church Youth Group Leader Adult Interviewee B said that young people being involved in sexual relations exposed themselves to many "risks such as: pregnancy, abortion, STDs, fear, shame, disrespect, sterility and abuse."

Both church based and the non church based youth group leaders agreed that schooling started sexual education too young and most females are taught now at age 9 yrs old about sex and having safe sex rather than abstaining. Both felt that by the time young people are in youth groups that most of their young people were involved to some degree in sexual relations.

The church based youth groups believe that their young people were less involved in sexual relationships than the non church based groups. My findings taken from the questionnaires is that there is minimal difference and that both groups of young people are actively involved in sexual relationships.

The non church based youth groups felt that young peoples relationships can provide a training ground for them to develop interpersonal skills. Through their dating relationships, young people often develop communication and negotiation skills, develop empathy, and learn how to maintain intimate relationships. The emotional ups and downs associated with getting together and breaking up may also help young people develop important skills. While breakups may put some young people at risk for depression, they may also help young people to develop emotional resiliency and coping skills needed to handle difficulties later in life.

This is precisely what Barber & Eccles were talking about in their book of 2003 and saying that as adults we may not like or put value on the young peoples relationships, however for the young people it can be a major development time for them.

The young people involved in the church based youth groups said that religion is important to them and those who attended church based youth groups regularly had a significantly lower rate of pre-marital sexual relations when compared to peers who did not consider religion important and attended non church based youth groups. The pre-marital sexual relations rate of those who never attended church based youth groups was about seven times higher than those who attended regularly.

Additional Youth Organizations Influence

During the research all 32 young people were regular attendees of the youth groups that I met them at. Out of the 32 young people 50% were involved in Church based groups and 50% were involved in non church based groups. On top of these groups I wanted to know if they were involved in any other formal youth group or organization. See Fig 5 below.

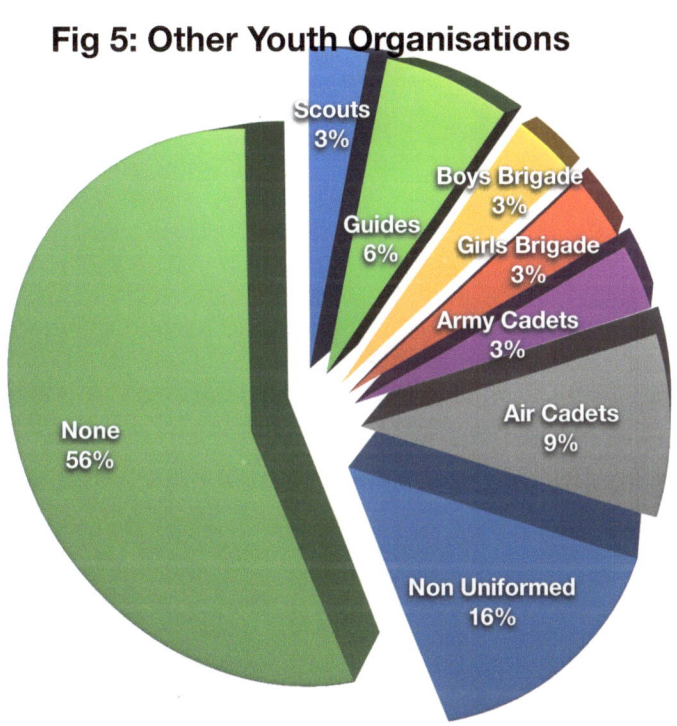

Fig 5: Other Youth Organisations

I was slightly surprised that the majority (56%) were not involved in other organizations and that the uniformed groups were not considered the most popular. The non-uniformed option was second most popular with 16% of the young people involved. I further developed this non uniformed option and the results are shown below. It seems the non uniformed groups that the 13% of the young people are involved with groups that are linked to their schooling or education with 3% involved in activity clubs. See Fig 6 below.

Fig 6: Non Uniformed Organisations

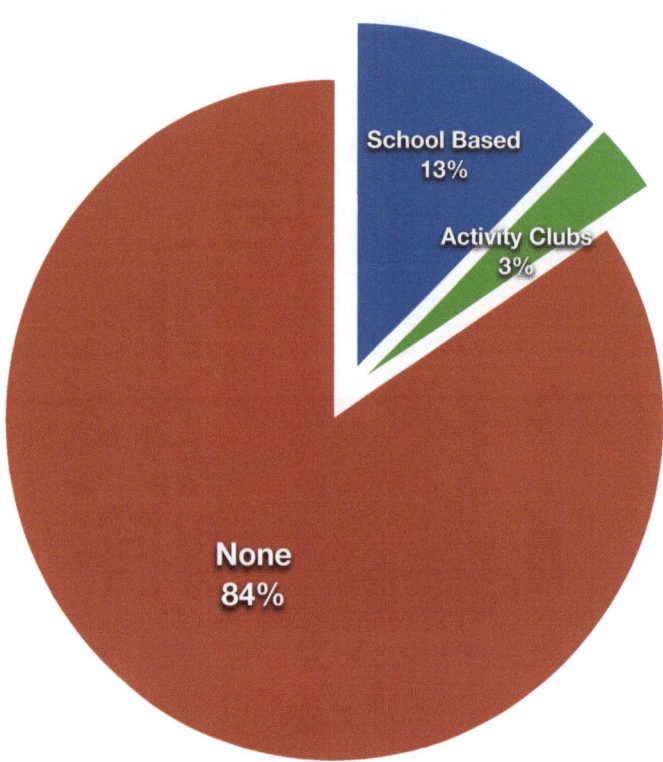

<u>Behaviors and Links to Crime</u>

The young people involved in church based youth groups hold more positive attitudes about life than do their less religious peers. The research revealed a statistical association between church based youth groups and less worries about life compared to young people who went to non church based youth groups at least once a week. See Fig 7 below.

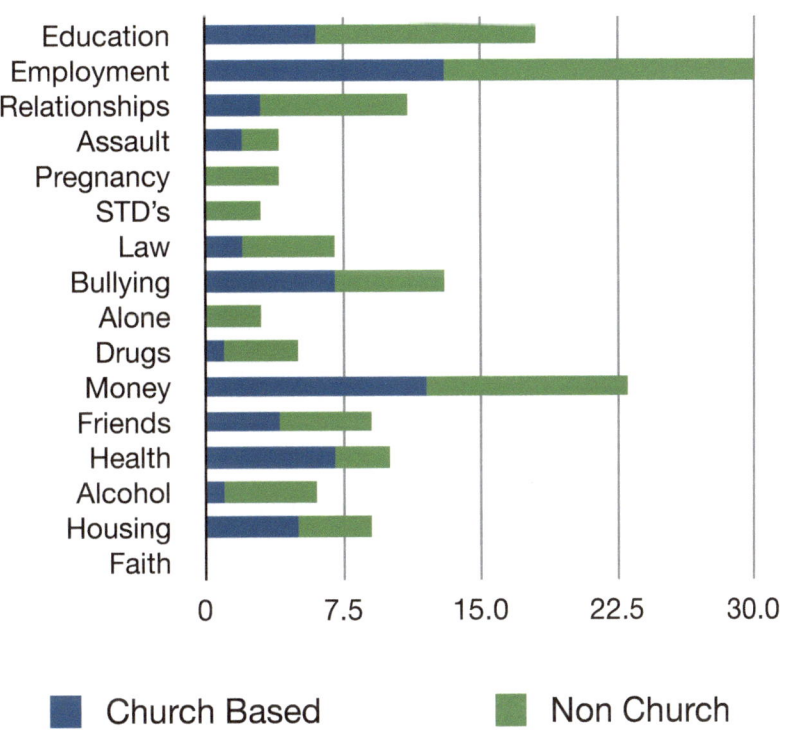

Fig 7: Comparison between Church based & Non church Based Youth Groups and what concerns them.

The young people involved in church based youth groups hold more positive attitudes about life than do their less religious peers. The research revealed a statistical association between church based youth groups and less worries about life compared to young people who went to non church based youth groups at least once a week. See Fig 7 above.

Interestingly both groups were concerned about employment and money with little difference between either group. There was a clear difference between Church based and non church based issues such as education, relationships, alcohol and sexual related issues with non church based youth being more concerned and worried about these issues. On the other hand the church based youth were more concerned about issues such as bullying, health and housing.

I found that all the young people who attended church based youth groups weekly said religion was very important to them were significantly more likely than non church based youth to have less worries in their lives and when I followed this up in their interviews the church based youth thought their lives were useful, felt hopeful about their futures, were satisfied with their lives and enjoyed being in school. I also found that young people involved with church based youth groups came from more stable and secure homes. However the non church based young people seemed to be quite nonchalant about life and the issues associated with it for them.

I now needed to know whether the young people felt the youth groups they were in were relevant to them and there lives.

Below we see a chart showing what the young people get out of their involvement in the youth group they are involved in.

Fig 8: What Young People Gain in the Youth Groups

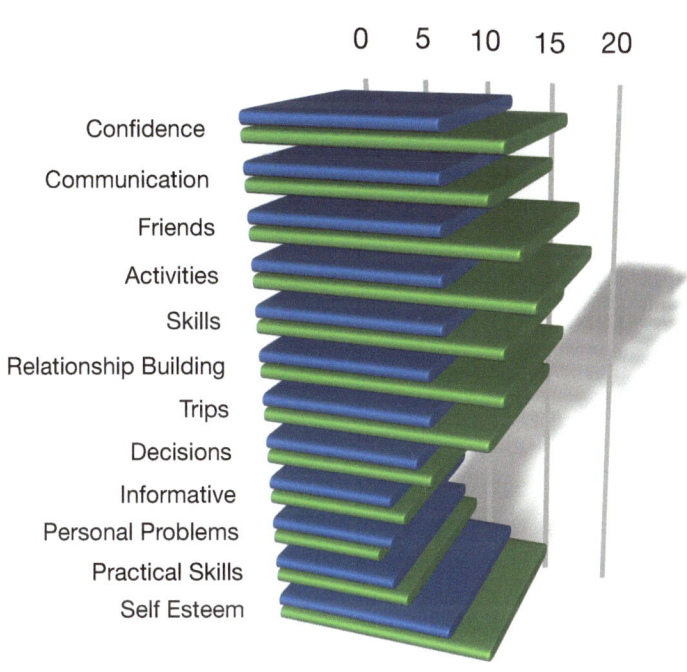

Confidence
Communication
Friends
Activities
Skills
Relationship Building
Trips
Decisions
Informative
Personal Problems
Practical Skills
Self Esteem

0   5   10   15   20

■ Church Based   ■ Non Church Based

Having spoken to 32 young people spread over two styles of youth group it would appear that non-church based youth groups are more beneficial to young people in all the above topics (see fig 8).

The only benefit we see that church based youth groups provide above non-church based youth groups is that of helping with personal problems. Because this research is an unbiased project I have not included specific issues such as development of faith because I believe that that would be an unfair and unrealistic response from either party as the church based groups include faith activities as part of their curriculum and the non church based groups do not include it so that wouldn't be a true reflection.

I wanted to know if the two groups benefited the young people by helping them avoid drug use, getting into trouble with police or the courts etc so I ensured questions were on my questionnaire about these specific subjects. The questions I asked them were;

1. How often you have tried each of these drugs in the last month?

2. Have you ever been involved in any of the following activities within the last year?

3. Have you ever been stopped or questioned by the police?

4. Have you ever been searched by the police?

5. Have you ever been in court or in front of the children's panel?

The results speak for themselves as shown below in fig 9;

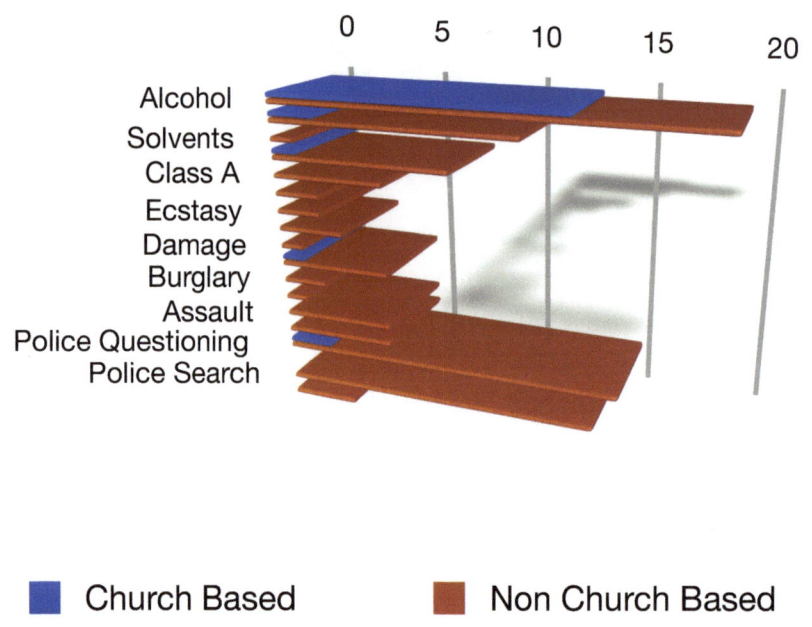

■ Church Based   ■ Non Church Based

Fig 9: Young People within the last month used or involved in;

Based on the results in fig 9, it would seem that the church based youth groups have more of an effect at helping young people _**not**_ get involved with Drugs, the police and the courts.

Whilst interviewing the young people it seemed that drugs are very easy to get hold of in school and college and that some of their older siblings do in fact deal in certain types of drugs. I asked whether they thought it was a bravado thing to do to get involved in drugs etc and they felt it was just a social thing to do and that everyone did it. On the subject of alcohol they said that it came down to going to mates and parties etc. Some of the young people stated that they could buy alcohol and cigarettes at any local shop easily as they were never asked for ID.

Chapter 5

Conclusion

The interviews I had with both leaders and the young people had a qualitative emphasis and the information gathered gives me an insight to the relevance of these groups in their localities from the non-young persons perspective.

Through these interviews I found that there is varied provision for young people. However it wasn't easy to see the effectiveness or relevance of all the provision as there is no central coordination of these groups in the localities. Examples of this included community education and uniformed organisations which have a presence but each locality had a different mix of 'traditional' youth work, sports groups, interest groups and uniformed organisations. There was also a diverse range of initiatives which have been developed by individuals or groups of people to meet what they see as the particular needs of young people in the locality. In some cases this provision was developed with the aim of tackling specific issues which are a cause for concern among adults in an area. My research suggested there maybe overlaps, and also some gaps in the provision for young people. However my primary focus for this research was church based and non church based youth groups.

I was surprised to see that some of the youth work leaders who completed forms for me were surprisingly vague and almost sarcastic in their responses. I was also surprised to see that the majority of their answers and responses were based around what they wanted for the young people rather than what the young people wanted or needed.

The church based groups provide provision in the areas that was specific to what they wanted or believed was right for the young people. It seemed from their questionnaires that the church based youth groups had youth agendas that they wrote for their young people. It also seems that the church based groups were controlled by church leaders, deacons and committees which either employ their youth group leaders or had members of the church to run the youth organizations.

The youth groups collectively agree that they are to provide a quality youth based facility, however it seems that the difference thereafter are stark. The Church based groups believe, and I quote Church Youth Group Leader Adult Interviewee A;

"To provide quality Christian based youth work that is both excellent, caring and effective in bringing about the churches vision".

As great as this may sound it doesn't mention anything about helping or benefiting the young people. This is not good as it means the focus is about the churches needs and agenda and not the young peoples.

In the same manner the non church based groups believe, and again I quote Non Church Youth Group Leader Adult Interviewee B,

"Our principles are to ensure the young people have a great time in a safe, youth centered program that enables the young people to flourish and reach their potential"

The difference is quite blunt. The church based groups don't mention the young people as their focus but mention their organizations agendas. The non church based groups talk about ensuring the young peoples needs are met. This is a contradiction to Jeffs and Smiths work of 1998.

I also found that variety was also found in the youth group leaders experiences, training and qualifications. It would seem that we had youth leaders with all the best will in the world with no qualifications running large youth groups and organizations, some of theses staff were extremely experienced, but no formal qualifications. Others were well qualified with minimal experience. This may make a difference to the youth groups but overall in this size study it wasn't very distinct and therefore isn't worth delving into in any further details.

One youth leader has been running groups for over 20 years is completely passionate about young people and helping them achieve their potential. He is absolutely sold out in his beliefs for them. However in his feedback we would find that the overall direction and plan of the youth work is not down to the young people or indeed him, but down to his board of governance within the church based group that he leads. When I asked about budgets the answers were vague and phrases like "a vision driven budget" were thrown out. This however doesn't allow for careful planning of activities and events as it is based on "vision" not "substance". This leader is paid full time by the church that the group is based in to achieve its goals.

Again the fact that the majority of youth workers nowadays are volunteers again shows that Tony Jeffs (2001) was right in his views that people are willing to give up their most valuable asset - Time, in order to support and help young people. The majority of non church based youth group leaders are volunteers and run the groups because of their passion for the young people. The church based youth group leaders were both in semi-paid positions and were selected because they believed it was an anointing that was put on their lives by God.

On the other end of the scale we have a non church based youth leader who again is completely passionate about the young people and helping them achieve their potential. Yet each year he has to apply for new funding from charitable organizations to ensure he can open the doors and pay the bills on the youth building he runs. He was receiving funding and support from the councils E3 scheme. However that is due to run out this summer due to political cutbacks so is now desperately looking for other funding. His focus is not on achieving a third party agenda but providing facilities and resources to keep the young people occupied and out of trouble.

I see that for both types of group there are obvious struggles. The influence these groups have on young people will stay with them for life and is crucial that both groups get it right. Some of these youth leaders have made it their career / vocation in life. Some of them have full time careers and running youth projects and organizations is something they do in addition. Either way it would seem that the managing of the youth groups is very different, with different agendas and goal sets. It would also seem that both groups want the young people to achieve their potential, however the main differences would be one is centered around achieving their organizations goals and the other is centered around the young people. However what is clear is that politics controls both regardless of anything else.

Within the churches it is the leadership of the church that controls the budgets and the staffing so they will do what ever they have to do to comply with that, even though it maybe subconsciously complied with. With the non church based groups they too are tied to politics as shown with the E3 funding which is due to run out this year. That funding came with guidelines and stipulations that the youth group must abide by to ensure they got the funding in the first place and report back to the E3 coordinators the progress and development of the group as a result of the funding. So with all the best intentions in the world both youth groups are somewhat managed and controlled by potentially good people who are really puppets in the bigger scheme of things all tied into funding.

I have tried to describe the methods I used to evaluate the relevance of youth work within church based and non church based groups of young people. A comparison between the selected areas and national statistics on unemployment and deprivation justifies my choice of areas. Information from the questionnaires provides further justification by showing that young people from single parent families and from homes without a full-time wage earner are overrepresented in this research. Moreover, my survey suggests that these young people are indeed vulnerable and in need of extra curricular support and help.

It would seem to me that neither youth group differs too much from each other. The young people who say they are involved in a church based youth group seem to be very similar to the young people who say they attend non church based youth groups. The main difference it would seem is that when it comes to serious issues such as drugs, and more serious crimes the non church based youth groups young people have been involved a lot more than the others.

Youth group based in the churches I met with have told me that it is not the same today as it was 10 or 20 years ago. They said that it started out originally for the sole purpose of teaching youth to read the Bible, but it has evolved into a ministry for teaching youth a lifestyle for Christ. Although the mission is to develop disciples for Christ, youth leaders seem to be losing many youth to the ways of the world.

The non church based groups lures the youth to them, and it seems more appealing to the teenage mind then Christianity. Church based youth groups may have some of the same motives it did 300 hundred years ago, but today they say they are working at digging deeper and changing the life of young people. They say they don't just want to change their life for four years, but for eternity. The church based youth groups mission should not be to have a mega church of youth, but to have a church that has numbers that stay for the long haul. It is true that many of the passionate youth they may work with today may disappear, and not choose to follow Christ in the future.

This shows that church based and non church youth groups do not do any justice to the work that the churches intellectual and spiritual heritage has helped to progress and expand the social sciences and human experience.

From the minimal research I have completed I cannot make judgements on such huge issues apart from to say that the perspective of Church based youth work approach and Christian heritage have nothing to give young people from a non church based background is not true, and on the contrary this church based approach may not only help young people grow physically but also mentally and spiritually as well with out any type of discrimination.

As can be seen from above in practice and delivery of Church based youth work promotes the same elements as generic youth work there is no contradiction. The main difference appears to be the addition of a faith in the church based youth groups.

With the findings from this study, I hope that both the church based and the non church based youth groups will have a better idea on where to focus their attention in order to attract and sustain youth involvement in their local areas and stay relevant to the young people. These facts may also serve as an encouragement to the leaders of the groups that they are all on the same sort of wave length with the main difference being faith.

On the side of what they got out of attending youth groups, since most of the youth chose gaining confidence, friends and doing activities as their top reasons for being involved, the youth groups can innovate programs and activities that will make use of this information and would suit the spiritual, emotional and physical needs of the youth of today.

So back to the question at the beginning of the research: are these youth groups relevant to the young people who attend them?

It would seem that yes they are. It would appear that the youth groups are relevant to their young people and have helped them develop in life skills, albeit they may be soft skills such as communication, self esteem, relationship building and helping them with life issues. However it also seems that when it comes to helping the young people maintain good and balanced lifestyles outside of the youth groups the church based youth groups are more relevant to the young people than the non church based youth groups.

Chapter 6

List of References

A. Fahmi, Mabadi'al-Tarbiya al-Islamiyya, (1999) Cairo, Lajnat al-Ta'lif wal-Tarjama wal-Nashr, 1366 AH,p. 148-50

Abd a-Wahid Wafi. (1957). The Prolegomena of Ibn Khaldun. 3 vols. Paris.

Ahmad, A. (1968). The Educational Thought of Ibn Khaldun. Journal of the Pakistan Historical Society (Karachi), Vol. XIV, p. 175-81.

Anderson, F. & Worsley, R. & Nunney, F. & Maybanks, N. & Dawes, W. (2009) Youth Survey Research study. Youth Justice Board for England and Wales.

Barber, B. & Eccles, J. (2003). The joy of romance: Healthy adolescent relationships as an educational agenda. In P. Florsheim (Ed.), Adolescent romantic relations and sexual behavior: theory, research, and practical implications. Mahwah, NJ: Lawrence Erlbaum Associates.

Beilin, H. (1994). Jean Piaget's enduring contribution to developmental psychology. A century of developmental psychology (pp. 257–290). Washington, DC US: American Psychological Association.

Bell, J (2005) Doing your research project: a guide for first-time researchers in education, health and social science. McGraw-Hill International

Berg, F (2001) Children and teens afraid to eat: helping youth in today's weight-obsessed world. University of California.

Brew, J, M. (1957) Youth and youth groups. Faber, London.

Bryant, D. (2008). The Failure of Youth. Retrieved May 7, 2010, from http://donbryant.wordpress.com. Accessed on 13th January 2012.

Catholic News Agency (http://www.catholicnewsagency.com/news/church-is-depending-on-youth-writes-benedict-xvi-in-wyd-2011-message/) Accessed on 30th January 2012.

Connolly, J., Craig, W., Goldberg, A., & Pepler, D. (2004). Mixed-gender groups, dating, and romantic relationships in early adolescence. Journal of Research on Adolescence, 14(2), 185–207.

DiGiacmo J & Wakin E. (1972). We Were Never Their Age. Holt, Reinhart and Winston, New York

Doyle, M, E. & Smith (1999) Born and Bred. Leadership, heart and informal education, London: YMCA

Fields D. (1998). Purpose Driven Youth Ministry. Zondervan Publishing House, Grand Rapids Michigan

Furman, W. (2002). The emerging field of adolescent romantic relationships. Current Directions in Psychological Science 11(5), 177- 180.

Furman, W., & Schaffer, L. (2003). The role of romantic relationships in adolescent development. In Florsheim, P. (Ed.), Adolescent romantic relations and sexual behavior: theory, research, and practical implications. Mahwah, NJ: Lawrence Erlbaum Associates.

Gomez F. (1986). The Filipino Youth: A Sociological Study. Social research Center, UST

Graham B. (1971). The Jesus Generation. Zondervan Publishing House, Grand Rapids Michigan

Hawthorne, A. (1999) Get God 2000. Marshall Pickering.

Haynes, N. & Ben-Avie, M & Ensign, J. (2003) How social and emotional development add up. Teachers College Press.

http://www.ewtn.com/wyd2000/background/10manila.htm Accessed on 13th January 2012.

http://www.statswales.wales.gov.uk/TableViewer/tableView.aspx?ReportId=430 Accessed on 13th January 2012.

Ibn Abi Usaybica (IAU), cUyun al-Anba, Cairo, al-Matbaca al-Wahhabiyya, 1299 AH, Vol. II, p. 2.

Ibn Sina, al-Najat, (2001) Cairo, al-Babi al-Halabi, 1357 AH, p. 158; and al-Shifa, Tehran, Hajar, 1353 AH, Vol.I, p. 294.

Jeffs, T, and Smith, M. K. (1998) 'Youth' in M. Haralambos (ed.) Developments in Sociology Volume 14, Ormskirk: Causeway Press, pp. 55-79.

Jeffs, T. (2001) 'Schooling, education and children's rights' in B. Franklin (ed) Children's Rights. London: Routledge.

Kelly G.A. (1962). The Catholic Youth's Guide to Life and Love. Random House, New York

Kitab al-Ibar (1867) The Book of Advice. Ed. by N. Hurini. 7 vols. Cairo, Bulaq

Krieger, B, J. (1996) Dialogue and Discovery New York: St.Martins Press.

Larson E. (1968). Good Old Plastic Jesus. Liguorlan Books.

Manaloto B. (1995). Youth Involvement in Parish.

Muqaddima Ibn Khaldun (1999) Ibn Khaldun's Introduction to History. 4 vols. Cairo.

Pope John Paul II, 10th World Youth Day. January 15, 1995.

Senter, M. H. (2010). When God Shows Up: A History of Protestant Youth Ministry in America. Grand Rapids, MI: Baker Academics .

Shelton C. (1989) Morality and the Adolescent: A Pastoral Psychology Approach. Crossroad, New York.

Smith, M. (1988) Developing Youth Work. Informal education, mutual aid and popular practice, Milton Keynes: Open University Press.

Smith, C. & Christoffersen, K. & Davidson, H. & Herzog, P, S. (2011) Lost in Transition: The Dark Side of Emerging Adulthood.

Strommen M. (2000). Passing on the Faith: A Radical New Model for Youth and Family Ministry. St. Mary's Press, Minnesota.

Strommen, Merton & Jones, Karen. (1973) Youth Ministry That Transforms: A Comprehensive Analysis of the Hopes, Frustrations and Effectiveness of Today's Youth Workers. Zondervan Publishing House, Grand Rapids Michigan.

Sweatman, A. (1879) The Church of England in Canada: extracts from the first charge. Church of England Press. London.

Teenage Research Unlimited (2006). Teen Relationship Abuse Survey. Liz Claiborne Inc. Retrieved January 29, 2012 from www .loveisnotabuse.com/pdf/ Liz%20Claiborne%20Mar %2006%20Relationship%20Abuse%20Hotsheet.pdf

Whittaker, N. (2000) A Philosophy of Youthwork in Practice. University of Minnesota.